D1199254

YOUNG PEOPLE'S STORY OF
OUR HERITAGE

YOUNG PEOPLE'S
STORY OF
OUR HERITAGE

EUROPE

by

V. M. HILLYER and E. G. HUEY

New Edition Designed and Revised by Childrens Press, Chicago

Consultants

William T. Nichol, Principal
Charles Gates Dawes Elementary School, Evanston, Illinois

John R. Lee, Professor of Education
Northwestern University, Evanston, Illinois

Meredith Press, New York

Illustrations in the order in which they appear

Library of Congress Catalog Card Number: 66-11334

Copyright © 1966 by Meredith Publishing Company. Originally published under the title of *A Child's Geography of the World* by V. M. Hillyer. Revised and Enlarged Edition, with new material by Edward G. Huey. Copyright, 1929, by The Century Co. Copyright, 1951, by Appleton-Century-Crofts, Inc. Copyright, 1957, by Mercantile Safe Deposit and Trust Co. All rights reserved. Printed in the U.S.A. Published simultaneously in Canada.

Contents

Acknowledgments

Cover drawing, top: Grapes used to make wine
John Hollis—Hollis Associates

Cover painting, bottom: Ships in busy European port
John Hollis—Hollis Associates

Page 2: Odense, Denmark, Birthplace of Hans Christian Andersen
Pan American Airways

Frontis: Guardsmen in London, England
Sabena Belgian World Airlines

Opposite: Finnish Lapp
General Consulate of Finland

———————————

Designer: Marita Kling

Project Editor: Joan Downing

*Editorial Staff: Frances Dyra,
Mary Reidy, Gerri Stoller*

EUROPE

The Continent of Europe

Europe is a small continent with about twenty-five countries. If you look on the map you will see that it has more shoreline than any other continent. There are also many river waterways in Europe. The Danube rises in the Black Forest of Germany and flows east to the Black Sea.

A thousand years before Columbus sailed west across the Atlantic, invaders from the East went up the Danube. Ruins of old castle forts can still be seen along the river. This is true of many rivers in Europe.

Other rivers in Europe flow west, north, and south. Even landlocked countries in Europe are not far from the sea.

Europe is not surrounded by water. In the east, the continent of Europe joins Asia. A big narrow plain, cut by the English Channel, lies across northern Europe. This plain becomes broader as it spreads across Russia.

South of the plain are highlands with their rivers and pleasant valleys. Then the Alps lift snowy peaks that separate the continent. The Pyrenees (peer'eh-neez) Mountains fence off the peninsula that is Spain. The Apennines (ahp' eh-nynz) straggle down the boot of Italy.

The rivers and the seas have always been important to Europeans as the waterways on which they traveled.

Before the time of Columbus, Europeans thought that the Atlantic Ocean was something like a river along their shores. They traveled on it and fished in it, but they didn't dare go far out on it. They thought they might fall off the edge of the world if they did.

The most courageous of the explorers were interested in how far the oceans spread. They were all looking for trade routes to other parts of the world.

Columbus found that there are 3000 miles of Atlantic Ocean between Europe and the Americas. It took him more than a month to sail across it. Now jet planes fly across the Atlantic in a few hours. Liners and freighters steam across it in a few days.

The oceans of the world are still broad highways for trade routes, but they are much more. Now we know that oceans cover about three-quarters of the earth. They affect the land in many ways.

Oceans are always moving. Twice each day the oceans move toward the land and away from it. This movement of the whole body of water toward the land and away from it is called *tides*. Tides are caused by the pull of the sun and the moon on the water.

There are streams called *currents* that flow like rivers through the oceans. The Gulf Stream in the Atlantic is almost a hundred miles wide and more than a mile deep. It is a stream of *warm* water that affects the climate of Great Britain and northern Europe. It is not a single river, but has branches running into it.

The Gulf Stream, with a color of its own, is a *surface stream*. There are also *cold* currents crossing and crisscrossing deep within the ocean.

The trade routes on the ocean surface have already been charted, and now the ocean floor is being mapped. In the ocean floor are mountains and deep valleys. There are level plains and deep crevasses. Food fish live in waters near the surface, and other water animals live at different depths. Plants grow in the oceans where sunlight filters through the water to them.

Europe is the center of Western civilization. All the countries of the New World had their beginnings there.

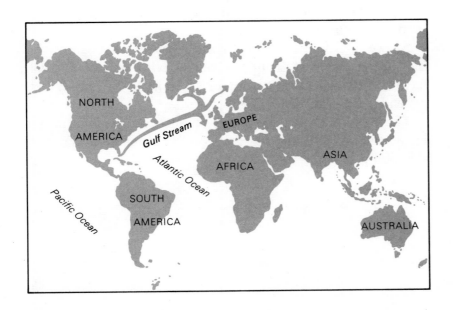

Map of the world showing the Atlantic Gulf Stream that affects the climate of Great Britain and northern Europe

For hundreds of years the people of Europe have advanced civilization. There are, of course, good reasons for this.

One reason is water. The surrounding seas and the rivers provide moisture for rain. Water is no problem for farmers of Europe. Industry uses water, too. Europe has enough water for both farming and industry. There are many good harbors in the irregular coastline of Europe. You would expect Europeans to be good sailors, and they are. Europe is located in a perfect spot for trading by sea. It is this location that has made Europeans masters of the sea. Great seamen, courageous enough to explore the world, have set sail from European ports.

The waters around Europe have provided fish for food, and fishing is still an important business in Europe.

Another reason that civilization has advanced in Europe is the climate. Europe is in what we call the *temperate zone*. There are few extremes of cold or heat. As we have said, no part of Europe is far from the sea, and the sea helps to moderate the climate.

Europe has its share of natural resources. There are vast amounts of coal and other minerals. There are rich farm lands and forests.

As we mentioned, there are about twenty-five countries in Europe. Some of them are very small. Not all of them have the same natural resources, so in some ways they are dependent on each other.

The ways in which the people of the countries of Europe have used the land and its resources is an important part of this story.

The Countries of Europe

There are enough countries in Europe to confuse you. In fact, it is probably safe to say that there are some countries in Europe that you have never heard of at all. As a start at sorting them out, we will group the countries in regions.

In *western and central Europe* are the United Kingdom, Ireland, France, Belgium, Luxembourg, the Netherlands, East Germany, West Germany, Switzerland, and Austria.

The countries of this region have played the largest part in the modern world. Industrious people in a pleasant climate have used their resources wisely. These countries are the workshop of Europe.

Northern Europe contains Norway, Sweden, Denmark, Finland, and that island by itself, Iceland.

They have many things in common. The sea, more than the land, dominates life in these rugged countries.

Spain, Portugal, Italy, and Greece make up *southern Europe.*

These are the warmest countries of Europe. Western civilization began in ancient Greece. Italy, in the time of the Roman Empire, did much to develop laws. Magnificent seamen from Spain and Portugal were the early explorers who mapped the world. These countries all have mountainous coastlines and warmth from the sea.

The countries of *eastern Europe* are Poland, Czechoslovakia, Hungary, Yugoslavia, Albania, Romania, Bulgaria, and part of the U.S.S.R. (home of the Russian people). The first six have been called the "Shatter Belt" because through the years the land that belongs to them has been fought over and split up. Now all six are Communist countries, associated with Russia.

The countries of Europe and their capitals:

COUNTRY	CAPITAL
Albania	Tiranë
Austria	Vienna
Belgium	Brussels
Bulgaria	Sophia
Czechoslovakia	Prague
Denmark	Copenhagen
Finland	Helsinki
France	Paris
East Germany	East Berlin
West Germany	Bonn
Greece	Athens
Hungary	Budapest
Iceland	Reykjavi
Ireland	Dublin
Italy	Rome
Liechtenstein	Vaduz
Luxembourg	Luxembourg
Monaco	Monaco Ville
Netherlands	Amsterdam and The Hague
Norway	Oslo
Poland	Warsaw
Portugal	Lisbon
Romania	Bucharest
San Marino	San Marino
Spain	Madrid
Sweden	Stockholm
Switzerland	Bern
United Kingdom	London
U.S.S.R.	Moscow
Yugoslavia	Belgrade

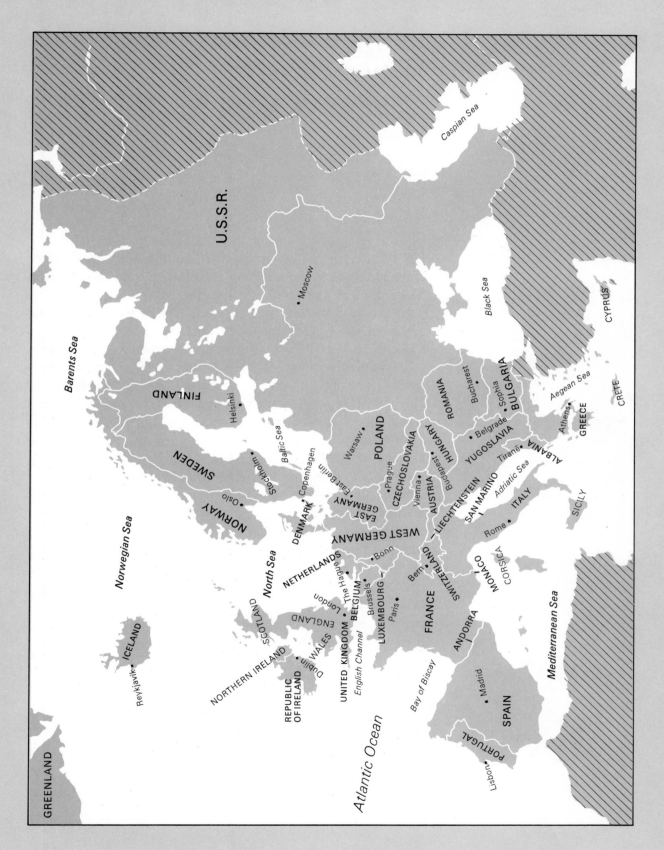

GREENLAND

Barents Sea

U.S.S.R.

Caspian Sea

Moscow •

Black Sea

CYPRUS

Norwegian Sea

FINLAND

Helsinki •

CRETE

Aegean Sea

BULGARIA

ROMANIA

Bucharest •

Sophia •

Athens •

GREECE

SWEDEN

Stockholm •

Baltic Sea

Warsaw •

POLAND

CZECHOSLOVAKIA

HUNGARY

Budapest •

Belgrade •

YUGOSLAVIA

Tiranë •

ALBANIA

NORWAY

Oslo •

Copenhagen •

Prague •

Vienna •

AUSTRIA

LIECHTENSTEIN

SAN MARINO

Adriatic Sea

ITALY

SICILY

DENMARK

East Berlin •

EAST GERMANY

WEST GERMANY

Rome •

North Sea

NETHERLANDS

Bonn •

The Hague •

SWITZERLAND

Bern •

MONACO

CORSICA

Mediterranean Sea

ICELAND

SCOTLAND

ENGLAND

London •

Brussels •

BELGIUM

LUXEMBOURG

Paris •

FRANCE

ANDORRA

Reykjavik •

NORTHERN IRELAND

WALES

Dublin •

UNITED KINGDOM

English Channel

REPUBLIC
OF IRELAND

Bay of Biscay

Atlantic Ocean

Madrid •

SPAIN

PORTUGAL

Lisbon •

Western and Central Europe

On the fertile plains with their rolling hills, the people learned to use the land. They fertilized the soil to renew it. They rotated the crops so that the same crop year after year would not wear out the soil. They raised sheep and cattle in the grassy mountain valleys. About half of the agricultural products of Europe come from these countries.

Perhaps the pleasant climate made these people energetic. Long ago, these countries became the *workshop* of Europe. The people made things of glass and metal and wood. They learned to use coal and steam for power. The countries became the industrial centers of Europe. These are the countries rich in fertile soil and coal and iron and forests. The people used their natural resources wisely.

The countries on the sea do about half of Europe's fishing. They have about three-quarters of Europe's commercial boats. With so many ships and so much to sell, these countries control the trade of Europe. Ships go to all parts of the world. The sailors learned long ago to use the prevailing winds and the currents in the oceans. When they sailed to faraway lands, they took with them ideas and customs of their countries. This is why they have played such an important part in the modern world.

opposite: A grain field in Flanders, Belgium

The United Kingdom
and Ireland

The British Isles are to the north of France. Two countries are there: the United Kingdom and Ireland. The United Kingdom takes up the whole of the larger island and a small part of the smaller island. England, Wales, Scotland, and part of Ireland (Northern Ireland) on the smaller island, make up the United Kingdom.

The Republic of Ireland is sometimes called Eire.

The British Isles are tiny compared to the rest of the land in the world. But for four hundred years the people were leaders of the world. How could this be?

For one thing, the British Isles are located in what we might call the "center of the world." There are good natural harbors from which ships could go to the New World and to other countries of Europe. Trade became important business.

The British Isles have many natural resources. They are surrounded by water. They have good farmland and a climate that is excellent for growing things. There are minerals under the ground, including coal. There is iron, too. So the United Kingdom is one of the European countries producing steel and products made from steel.

England is an old, old country, as are all the countries of Europe, the Old World.

When you think that it was only a little over three hundred years ago that the Pilgrims landed at Plymouth Colony, you can see why the Americas are called the New World. People were coming to England more than two thousand years ago.

It is no wonder that these islands were so attractive to invaders. The climate was pleasant. The woods were full of game. Rivers wandered through pleasant valleys in the Midlands. Surrounding waters were full of fish. Good harbors and snug coves dotted the shoreline.

London was a small village on the Thames River when Julius Caesar came with his army to claim the lovely island as part of the Roman Empire. This was fifty-five years before Christ was born. Some of the old walls the Romans built can still be seen.

Five hundred years later, Germanic people—the Jutes and Saxons—invaded the Island. These people were called *Angles*, (not to be confused with angels). The land was called *Angleland* from these people, and came later to be *England*.

A man named Arthur was a king at about this time. Have you ever read stories of King Arthur and his Knights of the Round Table? Many wonderful legends grew from this colorful time.

Other stories are told about a time five hundred years later in England's history. These are the stories of Robin Hood in Sherwood Forest.

In all this long time, people continued to live in much the same way. They farmed small plots of fertile land; they fished; they raised a few animals for food; and they hunted through the forests. Cloth for clothes was woven at home from wool or *flax*. Clay and metals were worked by hand to make pottery and tools.

For protection, the farmers lived together in little villages. They and their farms were protected by the lord of the manor. There are still many quaint and charming villages in England.

below: The tiny village of Leighton, England

About a hundred years ago something happened that changed the way of living in England, and in the whole world. Machinery was invented. Mills were built to weave cloth. Factories were built and things were produced by machines. Many people moved from farms and villages to work in the factories, and cities sprang up. People were paid for working in the factories. They used the money to buy the things they needed, instead of making these things themselves. This was a new way of living. It changed so many things that we call it the *Industrial Revolution*. The same thing has happened in all other countries, but it happened in England first.

Textile manufacturing is still an important industry in the United Kingdom. Cloth made in British mills is sold all over the world. Britain does not produce much silk, flax, cotton, or wool, so these raw materials for making cloth are bought from all over the world. Often the finished cloth is sold back to the country from which the raw materials came.

Come and visit London as the Romans did, by going up the Thames River. Englishmen pronounce this river the "temz" so perhaps we should call it that, too.

London is one of the biggest cities in the world. New York is a big city, too. New York is a tall city where buildings with fifty, seventy, or even a hundred stories climb to the sky. London is a broad city. It sprawls out over 600 square miles, and its buildings are not tall.

You can travel about London on a double-decked bus. Sitting on the top of the bus is a wonderful way to see the city and the people. These red buses have a partially open platform on the back. Some energetic people hop on and off this open platform before the bus comes to a full stop. You can ride an underground railway too but you do not see much of the city.

London is the capital of the country, and the place where laws are made is called the Houses of Parliament. This means "Houses of Talk." There is a royal family and a monarch, but the English people send men to Parliament to make their laws. A Prime Minister runs the country. The office of the Prime Minister is on Downing Street. This

opposite: Parade at the State Opening of Parliament

plain-looking building, with number 10 on the door guarded by a policeman, is the center of the British Empire.

There are tall, square towers on the Houses of Parliament. A huge clock in one of these towers is called "Big Ben." When it strikes it can be heard for a long way.

St. Paul's Cathedral was built more than three hundred years ago, after a fire called the "Great Fire" had burned most of London. Christopher Wren was the famous architect who designed this church, and many other buildings.

During World War II, thousands of buildings in London were destroyed by bombs dropped by the Germans during air raids. Many of Christopher Wren's churches were burned or smashed by the bombs, but he had built so many that there are still some left.

There is another famous church in London that Christopher Wren did not build. This church is very old. It is called Westminster Abbey. Westminster Abbey is not only a church, but also a tomb for famous people, the national shrine of England. Kings, queens, great writers, poets, musicians, and soldiers are buried here. Not only great people are buried here, but also a plumber, a prize fighter,

an actress, and a farmhand. After World War I, a soldier who had died on the battlefield in France, but whose name no one knew, was buried in Westminster Abbey to honor all those who had died without name or fame for a great cause. The place is called the Tomb of the Unknown Soldier.

In Westminster Abbey there is a chair in which all the kings of England sit when they are crowned. It is called the Coronation Chair. Underneath the seat of the Coronation Chair is a large stone. Why the stone underneath the chair seat? Well, hundreds of years ago the country north of England named Scotland was separate from England. When the kings of Scotland were crowned, they used a large stone for a seat. So when England and Scotland became one country, the people took the stone of Scotland and put it under the Coronation Chair of England, so that the king could sit on both seats while he was crowned king of both countries. The stone was stolen on Christmas, 1950, and taken to Scotland but is back in its place now.

The oldest group of buildings in London, built long before the Great Fire that destroyed most of London, is one which, from its name, sounds like only part of a building. It is called the "Tower." In times long ago the Tower itself was a prison. Many famous people—even princes and queens—were put in this prison, and some of them were put to death. Other buildings of the Tower of London are used as quarters where troops live.

The Tower itself is now a museum where you can see many interesting curiosities from those long-ago days. There are suits of armor that soldiers and their horses and even their dogs wore, the block and ax with which prisoners' heads were cut off, and wonderful jewels that the kings wore in their crowns—huge diamonds and rubies as big as walnuts. The queen's crown is there on a white satin pillow. It is studded with jewels, including a huge diamond called the "Koh-i-noor," which means "mountain of light." This stone was supposed to bring bad luck to any man who owned it, so a woman now owns it—the queen. The guards of the Tower are called "beefeaters." Should anyone break

opposite: Big Ben in London

into the cases in which the jewels are kept, the doors and gates of the Tower would automatically clang shut and the thief would be caught as a prisoner. The beefeaters' scarlet, black, and gold uniforms date back to medieval times but were brought up to date with Queen Elizabeth's insignia on the front. They are the guards of the Tower and also the guides. The beefeaters escort tourists through the Tower and tell all about the historical events that happened and are thought to have happened in the Tower.

Another old building in London is the Old Curiosity Shop. This tiny little shop was used as a setting for many of the novels written by Charles Dickens. It still is the same as it was in the early nineteenth century. It looks like a

country cottage, a little two-story store from yesterday. Inside souvenir objects can be bought on the ground floor and up the creaky staircase on the second floor. Inside and out it is really an Old Curiosity Shop.

Did you ever collect stones or stamps, butterflies or coins? Well, people have collected treasures and curiosities from all over the world and brought them together in a wonderful museum in London. This museum is the largest museum in the whole world. It is called the British Museum.

Another museum, the National Gallery, faces a famous square in London. Trafalgar Square, named after a famous naval battle in English history, teams with starlings and pigeons and people and fountains. In the center, on a tall column, stands a statue of Lord Nelson, the hero of the battle of Trafalgar, when Nelson defeated Napoleon's navy in 1805. Another building facing this square is St. Martin-in-the-Fields. This church is so called because when it was first built it was in the fields.

London policemen are called "Bobbies." This nickname comes from Sir Robert Peel, the Prime Minister who founded the metropolitan police system in the nineteenth century. These bobbies, or constables, are considered some of the finest police in the world, and they are also very courteous.

opposite: Trafalgar Square, London

---

right: A London Bobby

It is said that if all the streets in London were strung out in one line they would reach around the world. No one could ever know the names of all the London streets, not even the London bobbies, who are supposed to know most things about London. They are either so famous or so funny that people remember them. There are Threadneedle Street and Cheapside, Pall Mall and Piccadilly, where the fine houses, hotels, and clubs and palaces are. There are Fleet, Strand, Regent, and Bond Streets, which are shopping streets. Also there is Baker Street, the beat of the fictional detective Sherlock Holmes. There is Oxford Circus and Piccadilly Circus, but there is no "circus" there. A circus is simply a big open space where streets cross. They could be called "squares" or "circles."

On a walk down any of the famous streets you will see many different sights. Near the Pall Mall, where the clubs are located, men dressed in tails or morning suits can be seen going to lunch at their clubs.

More people in England live in London than anyplace else. But that does not mean that there are not many, many other cities and towns and villages in the land. Most people who live in the country get to London sometime in their lives and many of them who live outside London have jobs in that city. They usually travel to London by train.

Steam trains were invented by an Englishman, and now there is train service nearly everywhere in England. These trains have a special look to them. The trains are compact and the cars are divided into rooms. In each room half the seats face forward and half face backward. Some of these rooms are labeled "1st class" but most are "2nd class." People pay more to ride in a first-class room than they pay to ride in a second-class room. The first-class rooms are more comfortable and have fewer people. The English railroad trains run on the left-hand side of the road. Englishmen drive their cars on the left-hand side of the road, too.

If you were to drive along English country roads you would notice that most of them have hedges alongside. The hedges act as fences but are much prettier. Sometimes the hedges are like those that grew up around Sleeping Beauty's castle, so thick and so high that you cannot see through them or over them. The houses behind them are hidden, except perhaps the roofs.

Some of the roofs are quite different from most roofs you have seen. They are made of piles of straw which are called "thatch." You would hardly think thatched roofs would keep the rain out, but they do. And you would think that they would burn up easily, but they don't.

The houses themselves are seldom built of wood, because there is very little wood in England. Nearly all of them are built of stone or of brick. Why do you suppose there isn't much wood for houses in England, where there were once forests full of game? England is very old, and hundreds and hundreds of years ago the people cut and used the trees. The few forests that were left were made into parks. Trees are very valuable in any country that does not have many of them, and so in England a house made of wood would be very expensive.

People build their houses from material that is plentiful and easy to obtain. Pioneers in the wilderness of North America built their houses of logs that they cut from the trees of the forest. Eskimos sometimes build houses of ice blocks, and some more primitive peoples in the hot climates make them from grass. You can tell a lot about a country— about what its natural resources are—by looking at the houses the people live in. In England the houses are mostly stone and brick, so you know that that country has a lot of the natural resources that make bricks and they have a lot of stone as well.

England has many interesting churches and cathedrals besides St. Paul's and Westminster Abbey. Only a very few of them are less than a hundred years old. Many of the cathedrals are more nearly a thousand years old. Most of the people in England are Episcopalians, so most of the churches in England are Episcopal churches. In fact, the Episcopal Church is called the Church of England.

England has many famous universities as well as churches and cathedrals. Two of the greatest universities in the world are in England. They are called Oxford and Cambridge. Their names come from their locations. Oxford is on the River Thames at a place where oxen used to cross, or "ford," the river. That is why that university is called "Oxford." The other university is by the River Cam at a place where there is a bridge. So this university is named "Cambridge."

Many of the world's greatest writers, whose stories you read and whose poetry you have learned, lived in England. The greatest of them all was William Shakespeare. He lived in England at a place called Stratford-on-Avon.

above: Shakespeare's classroom, Stratford

If you go north from London through the pleasant rolling Midlands you will come to industrial England where factories darken the sky with smoke.

The farms of England no longer feed all the people. Much of the food for the country has to be brought in from other countries.

On the Thames just north of London, is Windsor. For more than 1000 years, Windsor Castle has been the residence of British Monarchs.

On the English Channel, just an afternoon's drive from London, is the city of Hastings. The year 1066 and the Battle of Hastings are very important in the history of England. William of Normandy, called William the Conqueror, defeated the English King Harold on a ridge near the city of Hastings. This ridge is now a little town called simply Battle. Hastings is now a modern resort town with the ruins of William the Conqueror's castle.

Wales is along the west coast of England and juts out toward Ireland. It was once an independent country, but is now a part of the United Kingdom. Wales is mountainous, and much of the land is good only for pastures. This was a poor country until its resources of coal and the industrial revolution brought it prosperity. Its narrow coastal lowlands are a resort area.

The people love music and poetry. Their lyrical language shows their love of music. Every year more than twenty-five countries compete in the International Eisteddfod where they perform folk singing and dancing.

In Wales there is a town with the longest name I know. It is Llanfairpwllgwyngyllgogerychwyrndrobwllllantysiliogogogoch. That looks as though we had been playing on a typewriter and had pounded out the letters at random. But it is a real name. People who live in Wales are called Welsh and they have a language of their own, although they also speak English. In Welsh, that long name we just gave you means "The Church of St. Mary, in a hollow of white hazel, near a rapid whirlpool near the Church of St. Tysilio, which is near a red cave." People who live in the town usually call this place simply "Llanfair P.G." for short.

opposite: Folk dancers at Wales' International Eisteddfod at Llangollen

England had a hard time conquering Wales, because the people were good fighters. But at last an English king did manage to take the country to the south and he made it part of his own. In order to make the Welsh people satisfied and happy he told them he would give them a ruler who was born in Wales and couldn't speak a word of English. The people in Wales were very pleased at that, for they thought the king would give them one of their own countrymen to rule over them. But the king's own son was born in Wales—of course he was a baby and he couldn't speak a word of English or of any other language either. So the king made him the ruler of Wales and called him the Prince of Wales. Ever since then, the King of England's firstborn son, the one who will be king when his father dies, has been called the Prince of Wales.

Just as the people in Wales were once independent of England, so were the people to the north independent. The country to the north of England is Scotland and the people are Scottish. They once had their own king but now the king of England is also the king of Scotland.

The *southern uplands* of Scotland form a natural barrier between Scotland and England. The *northern highlands* cover half of Scotland. The center of the country is low land with many river valleys. The coastline has towering cliffs and headlands, bays and inlets. There are fine harbors where the rivers meet the sea.

Scottish men used to wear—and some do today—shawls of bright-colored squares and skirts called *kilts* instead of trousers. They wore stockings that left their knees bare even in cold weather. And there is a lot of cold weather in Scotland! Scottish families are called clans and each clan has a special design called a *tartan*. Shawls and skirts are woven in these designs and the cloth is called a *tartan*, or plaid.

The Scots have a peculiar musical instrument called a bagpipe. It is a bag made out of a pig's skin and it has a pipe to blow it up as you would a balloon. Several horns are attached to the bag. The player puts the bag under his arm, keeps blowing it up to keep air in it, and at the same time

above right: Kilted Scots Guards parade near the Tower of London

below right: Scottish bowman takes aim

30

31

he squeezes out the air with his arms so that it blows the horns and makes a unique kind of music.

This instrument is quite an invention. So is a game that the Scottish people made up. It is golf. Did you know that the Scottish people invented the game of golf? It is played all over the world, because people of many countries like it.

Some of the great ships in the world are made in Scotland, at a place called Glasgow on the River Clyde. Edinburgh, on the east coast, is the capital.

The Presbyterian Church started in Scotland and most of the people who live in Scotland are Presbyterians, just as those in England are Episcopalians.

Scotland is a rugged country and much of the food for the people has to be brought in from other countries.

Northern Ireland is part of the United Kingdom, and is ruled by the King of England. In the country around the capital, Belfast, flax grows especially well. Flax is much stronger and silkier than cotton, and making fine linen from flax is an important industry. There is more linen made in Belfast than anywhere else in the world.

below: A thatched house in County Limerick, Ireland

Potatoes are a staple crop. In years when the potato crop fails, many Irishmen move to the New World.

Most of the people of Northern Ireland are Presbyterians like the Scots or Episcopalians like the English, for their ancestors many years ago moved to Northern Ireland from Scotland.

In Southern Ireland, an independent country called Eire, most of the people are Roman Catholic. The capital of Ireland, or Eire, is Dublin. It is the economic, educational, and cultural center of the Republic of Ireland. It is often said that the people in Dublin speak better English than even the people in England do. Another language once spoken in Ireland more than English was Irish, or Gaelic. This was used long ago by the ancient Irish people before they spoke English. Some of the Irish coins and stamps have Irish words on them. Even today Gaelic is taught in the schools.

Outside the cities of Ireland, in the little country villages, are found thatched-roof houses.

The people of Ireland are said to be wonderful storytellers. They love to tell exciting and romantic stories which quite often are exaggerated. Many people visit Blarney Castle and kiss the Blarney Stone to gain this power of speech and flattery.

You have heard of St. Patrick, who was supposed to have driven the snakes out of Ireland. St. Patrick is the patron saint of Ireland. The patron saint of Scotland is St. Andrew, and the patron saint of England is St. George. The British flag uses the crosses of each of these saints for its design.

Ireland gets plenty of rain so the country is beautiful and green. It is sometimes called the "Emerald Isle," because it is like a sparkling green jewel set in the sea.

right: A Northern Irish boy admires a bugler

British Travel Association Photo

France

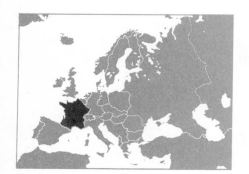

Distances are never great from country to country in Europe, for as we have said, the continent is a small one. A short boat trip will take you across the twenty-four miles of English Channel to France. It may be a rough crossing, for wind sweeps down the Channel, often making it choppy.

Another reason the Channel is often rough may be that it is not very deep. Around all continents there is an *underwater shelf*. This continental shelf around the British Isles and northern Europe is only 500 feet under water. Beyond the shelf, the Atlantic drops sharply to 10,000 feet.

Look at the map and you will see France reaching out a point of land toward England. In fact, France reaches out in all directions almost like a star in the heart of Europe. It extends in the south to the Mediterranean. Through the years of history, France was a kind of land bridge between lands on the Mediterranean and those in the north.

The west coast of France is on the Atlantic. Inland it borders Belgium, Luxembourg, Germany, Switzerland, and Italy.

France is a beautiful country with a pleasant climate.

Long rivers wind through beautiful valleys. The Seine (sane) flows to the English Channel. The Loire (lwahr) flows to the Atlantic. The Rhône rises in the heart of France and flows to the Mediterranean. In early days, sailors could go up the Rhône and down the Seine to get from the Mediterranean to the North Sea. Rivers were early waterways through the land. Now small boats and many barges with freight travel them.

France seems to have everything. There is enough fertile soil so that small farms can raise food for all the people. There are rolling hills and lovely valleys. There are snow-capped mountains on the Swiss border. Warm, sunny beaches along the Mediterranean are sheltered by mountains from cold northern winds.

opposite: Ile de la Cité with Notre Dame

France also has one of the loveliest cities in the world. Paris.

About 2,000 years ago, when Julius Caesar was crossing France, he came upon a little village on an island in the Seine. Caesar called these people "Parisii" and Paris got its name.

Now this capital city of France spreads for miles on both sides of the river. Many beautiful bridges span the river and link the city together.

If you cross one of them to the island in the Seine (Ile de la Cité), you will see a cathedral built about 800 years ago. It was built in honor of the Virgin Mary and is called Notre Dame, which in French means "Our Lady." It was built of stone and stained glass, and the walls are very thick.

The cathedral has two towers in front and a thin spire in the center. Long stone props give support to the roof. They are called "flying buttresses." If these props were taken away, the roof would tumble down.

Around the edge of the roof there are strange animals made of stone. They are hideous creatures—different from any real animals you have ever seen or heard of—part bird, part devil. These creatures are called *gargoyles*, and they were made as ugly as possible and put there on the edge of the roof because in the days long past it was thought that they would scare away evil spirits from the church.

French Government Tourist Office

There is another famous church in Paris built to honor Mary Magdalene. It is called "The Madeleine," for her. It is much newer than Notre Dame but it is older looking. It is built like the temples they used to build in old Roman times.

In a busy section of Paris is the opera house. This section has many sidewalk cafes and people sit for hours talking and watching the people pass. The outside of the opera house is richly decorated. But even all the rich decorations on the outside cannot prepare you for the elegance of the inside. White marble staircases lead to the foyer where glowing crystal chandeliers light the paintings and sculpture. For some performances, soldiers in full-dress uniforms line the staircase at attention while the audience enters in their finest clothes.

One of the most important buildings in Paris is not a church but a museum called the Louvre. There are many famous pictures and statues in the Louvre. A photograph is never worth much money, even though it may be a good likeness of a famous person. But a painting, even if it is not a good likeness of a person who is not famous may be worth a fortune. One of the greatest pictures in the world is in the Louvre. It is called the *Mona Lisa*.

Two of the most famous statues in the whole world are also in the Louvre. They were made in the days of the ancient world—when civilization was very young. One of them is a marble figure of the goddess *Venus*. The other is an angel with outspread wings. It is called *Victory*. The statue of *Venus* has lost her arms and *Victory* has lost her head, but, in spite of that both figures are more beautiful than most real people and they are very valuable. Of course, the Louvre has many, many more paintings than the *Mona Lisa* and many, many more statues than *Venus* or *Victory*. The Louvre was once a palace for French kings. Each king built more rooms on the palace until it became enormous. It has more than two miles of galleries.

Paris has many boulevards and avenues. One of the finest avenues in the world is in Paris. It is lined with trees and runs directly toward the setting sun. It was thought beautiful enough to be a street in Paradise, so it was called the Champs-Elysées (shahn-zay-lee-say') which means "The Fields of Paradise."

In London a square is called a "circus," but in Paris it is called a "place," pronounced "plass." The most beautiful

opposite top: The Champs-Elysées, Paris

opposite bottom: A sidewalk cafe, Paris

place in Paris is the Place de la Concorde. In the center of this place is a monument made of one single tall stone standing on end, an obelisk. It is called Cleopatra's Needle. On Friday and Saturday nights, lights illuminate the beautiful waters from the fountains, and this monument which is over 3000 years old. The Place de la Concorde is at one end of the Champs-Elysées and at the other end is a beautiful arch like a huge gateway across the avenue. It is called L'Arc de Triomphe, (lark' duh-tree-ahmf') which means The Arch of Triumph. Napoleon ordered the construction of this arch in honor of the French army. It is placed, according to Napoleon's orders, in such a way that the sun rises directly over the middle of the arch on Napoleon's birthday. The arch is set in a circle and from the top of the arch a view of the twelve streets that radiate from the circle can be seen. No automobile or carriage may pass through this Arch of Triumph, for underneath it in the pavement is the Tomb of the French Unknown Soldier.

For the Paris World Fair in 1889, Alexandre Eiffel built a gigantic tower. This 985-foot steel tower is now a landmark of Paris. Restaurants are on both the first and second landing of the tower and from the top on a clear day a distance of forty miles can be seen.

The French people love beauty in everyday things—in things such as hats and clothes and food and manners. French clothes are famous all over the world and set the fashion even in places thousands of miles away. French cooking is an art that is famous all over the world. Strangely enough, most French dress designers are men, and the great French cooks, the ones who cook for the great French restaurants, are men too.

Throughout France, and especially in Paris, dining is like nowhere else in the world. The food and service are both excellent. Usually the food is made to order. That is, it is not cooked until a customer orders it. This may take a long time but it makes the food delicious. French chefs take great pride in their work. In many small restaurants, the chef comes out from the kitchen to see if the customer is enjoying the food. To show appreciation, customers "send their compliments" to the chef. That is, they tell the chef how much they enjoyed his cooking. A famous cooking

opposite: The Eiffel Tower dominates the skyline of Paris

school, Cordon Bleu, teaches people from many lands the art of French cooking.

The French love the out-of-doors. Even in the cities they often eat their meals out-of-doors at sidewalk cafes. You can see them as you walk around the streets of the cities and towns.

Paris is in the center of a saucer-like basin. On farms around the city are raised vegetables and wheat and other grains. This part of France is the "breadbasket" of the country.

In the provinces of Brittany and Normandy, on the Atlantic, there are apple orchards and sleek cattle. The harbors along the rocky coast are full of fishing fleets. Peasants still wear native costumes in this quaint and colorful part of France.

Scattered through France there are wonderful vineyards where grapes are grown. Wine-making is an important business of the country.

There are other industries in France. One of the most important is textile making. Along the Rhône River the French people raise mulberry trees on which silk worms feed. Silkworms eat the leaves of the mulberry trees. After a silkworm has eaten, he spins a thread of silk, a quarter of a mile long, and wraps himself in it. If he broke out of this cocoon as a moth, the thread would be broken. So the worms are killed and the thread unwound. It is then woven into silk cloth. The city of Lyons (lee-ohn'), on the Rhône River, is a center of the textile industry.

Near the city of Grasse in southern France, acres and acres of flowers are raised for perfume. French perfume, made from real flowers, is famous all over the world. Tons of these flowers are needed to make small amounts of perfume. Visitors can see demonstrations that show part of the process for making perfume. But the important equipment and formulas are secret.

France has some iron and coal. Automobiles, machine tools, and electrical machinery are manufactured. But France is more a farming country than an industrial one.

French people do not manufacture as many things as do some other countries, but they are proud of their craftsmanship.

As you travel through France you are reminded constantly that this is part of the Old World. There are old castles from which knights in armor once rode off to battle.

There are lovely chateaus (shaa-toes') along the Loire Valley. These are a little less grim than earlier castles that were also forts. Many of the chateaus were built about the time that Columbus was setting out to prove that the world is round.

In the foothills of the Pyrenees Mountains that separate France from Spain there are caves where early man painted pictures on the walls 15,000 years ago.

The River Rhône flows south into a gulf called the Gulf of Lyons, which is a part of the Mediterranean Sea. The chief city of the Gulf of Lyons is Marseilles (mahr-say'). It is the next largest city in France after Paris, but it was a city long before there was any Paris, for it was a port for ships that sailed the sea long, long ago. It still is one of the great ports. Marseilles is very near the mouth of the Rhône, the place where it empties into the gulf.

The French Riviera is the low southern section of France bordering the Mediterranean Sea. Rows of mountains just behind the coastline protect this area from the cold northern winds. Soft sandy beaches, clear blue water and sky, and year-round blossoms make the Riviera ideal for vacation. Many people come to this area to enjoy some relaxation in the warm sun.

left: The Port of Marseilles

Belgium, The Netherlands and Luxembourg

Belgium is a small country between France and the Netherlands. It is on the narrow plain that lies across Europe. Belgium is hilly on the side near France, but on the opposite side it is very low. On this low side it joins the land of Holland, or the Netherlands. Belgium is not, however, as low as the Netherlands on the north, nor as high as tiny Luxembourg that lies in the hills to the southeast.

Warring neighbors of Belgium have fought battles on its land. The land of Luxembourg was too high, and the Netherlands were so low the dikes could be opened to flood an invading army. But Belgium was easy to cross, and many times this little country had to rebuild after armies fought across its land.

The seaports of Belgium and the Netherlands connect with a network of canals, rivers, and railroads. These countries are the crossroads of a great trading area.

Belgium has been called the land of bells and battlefields. The bells are in the towers of churches, town halls, and other buildings. The bells in Belgium strike the hour, but they do more than that—they play a tune every hour or oftener. And on Sundays and holidays a bell-ringer, seated at a keyboard, plays all sorts of hymns and tunes on the bells, so that everyone in the town can enjoy the music without leaving his own home. Thus the music is broadcast without a radio.

Some of the bell sets have as many as fifty bells of different sizes and sounds—little bells that make high notes, and big bells, as big as a man that make deep, low notes. The bells themselves don't move. The bell clapper moves instead. The clappers are fastened by wires to keys

opposite top: A tempting offer of waffles

opposite bottom: Fishermen catching shrimp on horseback

like those of a piano or an organ, and as the player touches the keys, the clappers strike the sides of the bells. When a bell concert is being given, all noises in the streets are forbidden.

The capital of Belgium is Brussels. Perhaps you have heard of Brussels lace, Brussels carpets, or Brussels sprouts. They all come from Brussels.

Waffles are a delight in Belgium. In cities like Brussels they can be bought on the street with paper wrappers so you can eat them as you walk along.

Brussels has many beautiful old sections with large squares surrounded by beautiful Gothic buildings. Modern buildings and roadways have also been built.

Another city of Belgium beginning with a "B" is Bruges (broozh). Bruges has many streets of water with bridges crossing them and boats instead of cars, although there are paved streets there, too.

Summer resorts in Belgium cover a forty-mile stretch of sandy beaches along the North Sea. Many people from England ferry across for a weekend. From the ferry docks at Ostende, the Crusaders sailed to free the Holy Land from the Infidels. A little west of Ostende you can see fishermen using horses to catch shrimp!

The people of Belgium first became famous for the lace they made. Now coal has helped Belgium become an indus-

trial nation. Many businesses have grown from the fine skill of the home crafts.

There is some good dairy land in Belgium, so the country has milk and cheese. Cattle are raised as well as barley, oats, and potatoes. But Belgium has to import some of its food.

Luxembourg is a tiny country. It is only about thirty-seven miles across one way and sixty-two miles across the other. It is an independent country, a *Grand Duchy*, with a grand duke or grand duchess as ruler. A third of the country is forest and the land is too poor for farming. The whole country is crisscrossed with rivers and deep valleys.

Tiny as it is, Luxembourg's place in industry is not small. There is much iron and coal, and half the people in the country make their living in manufacturing. Coal is exported to industrial neighbors.

The Netherlands is the official name of the country that we often call Holland. Holland is the name of just one province.

Holland means "hollow land." The country was named that because in many places it is even lower than the sea. Banks or walls called dikes had to be built to hold the water back. Windmills with big sprawling wings had to be built inside the dikes to pump the water out and keep it out. Water won't run off the ground in Holland, for there is no lower place for it to run to. It has to be pumped off from some of the lowest places.

The dikes that hold back the sea have to be big and very strong to stand the pounding of the waves against them. The slightest break or hole in the dike would soon burst open and the water would flood the country. So men watch the dikes all the time and mend any broken places as soon as they are made.

But long, long ago—about seven hundred years ago—there was a terrible storm and the North Sea did break through and flood villages and houses and drown thousands and thousands of people. Ships sailed and fish swam where this drowned village lay and this inland water was called the South Sea, which in Dutch is the Zuyder Zee. This is now called the Ijsselmeer. A nineteen-mile dike has re-

left: Windmills help irrigate the Belgian countryside

claimed part of it. Where most countries have roads and streets, the Dutch have canals. In the summer boats sail on the canals, and in the winter the people skate on them. Children skate to school and men skate to work.

In Holland there are not many horses. Dogs and bicycles are used to haul and carry. Dogs eat less than horses and they don't need stables. Bicycles don't need garages.

There are many cows in Holland so the people have a lot of milk from which to make cheese. The cheese is world famous. In the city of Alkmaar, from April to September, cheese auctions are held every Friday morning. Men in wide, colored hats carry the cheese in barges and toss the cheese around as bids are being taken.

The Dutch keep their houses very clean. The kitchen is usually the living room and dining room too. Dutch housewives scrub and scrub outside as well as inside. They scrub even the sidewalks and in some towns even the streets. The cow shed is often part of the house and is kept just as clean as the house.

There are still some places in Holland where you can see people wearing wooden shoes that they take off when they enter the house. And you can see the men wearing trousers as big as pillow cases, and girls wearing big skirts and white bonnets. In the large cities, however, the people dress about the same as they dress in other large cities of the world.

"Dam" means "dike" and as there are so many dikes in Holland there are many towns and cities that have names ending in "dam." Amsterdam is one of them. Amsterdam is the capital of the constitutional government, but the capital buildings are not there. They are at The Hague.

Amsterdam is a city of diamonds. The diamonds are not found in Holland but are brought there from Africa. When they are taken out of the diamond mines, they do not look like diamonds but like pebbles. You would never guess that they could be made into anything beautiful. But at Amsterdam they are made into the beautiful sparkling jewels that we know.

A diamond is the hardest thing in the world. You cannot cut it with a steel tool nor grind it on a grindstone. You cannot scratch it with sandpaper or make a mark on it with a file. The only thing that will cut a diamond or scratch it is another diamond. So in Amsterdam they chip one diamond with another diamond and use diamond dust to polish it.

45

Holland might be called the garden of Europe for it raises fruits and vegetables and flowers. Acres of tulips bloom in Holland and are a gorgeous sight. Tulip bulbs from here are sent all over the world.

Holland is a densely populated country, even though about two-fifths of its land is below the level of the sea. The plucky people of Holland have had to fight the sea for years. They continue to build dikes and dams and make more land available. When Julius Caesar came through Holland he found small farms where farmers had been fighting the sea for four hundred years.

In recent years almost 900 square miles of farmland have been reclaimed from the Zuyder Zee. It was so big an area that it was done in four sections. First, big dams were built. Then the water was pumped out of the four sections. Tracts of lowland reclaimed with dams or dikes are called *polders.*

opposite, top left: Porters at the Cheese Market, Alkmaar

opposite, top right: Bicycle riders in the Netherlands

opposite bottom: Amsterdam, the Netherlands

West Germany

The northern part of West Germany is sandy shore along the North Sea. This is a continuation of the Dutch lowlands. The land rises slowly to the central mountains, which are really worn-down uplands. The mountains of southern Germany merge with the high Bavarian Alps along the borders of Switzerland and Austria.

This is the land of the Black Forest, the Danube, the Rhine River. Wonderful stories of fairy-tale people and of real people who lived in the caves along the river or in the Black Forest have come to us from this land. The Brothers Grimm collected these tales told by the local peasants. Children and adults love to read them. Walking through the forest, you will not see the big bad wolf but you might see little girls wearing red hoods just like Little Red Riding Hood. Castles where Prince Charming or Sleeping Beauty might have lived dot the area.

On both sides of the Rhine are steep hills and rocks, and on top of these hills are castles built many years ago. The men who built them were called *robber barons*. They built their castles on these hills so that they could rob and still be safe from their enemies. The poor people, who lived down in the valleys, had to give part of what they raised to the barons. If they did not do so, the barons would swoop down on them with their men and take what they wanted and destroy the people's homes.

The people knew it was useless to attack the barons because of their strong castles. Most of these castles are now in ruins because it is too hard to get to them and to keep them in repair. No longer can anyone treat the poor people the way the barons treated them.

In 1949, after the division of Germany, Bonn was selected to be the capital of West Germany, which is officially called the German Federal Republic. Bonn is on the Rhine River.

The Rhine, which has its longest section in Germany, is used as a major waterway. Pleasure boats, ore boats, and freighters go up and down the river. Along the banks in some sections can be seen terraced vineyards. Terraces are flat sections of land, one above the other, that look like large steps. Here are grown grapes used to make Rhine wine, which is sold throughout the world.

Many bridges, old and new, cross the Rhine River. Both old and new bridges cross the Rhine at a city called Cologne. Cologne is a kind of perfume and was named after this city. Cologne means "colony." It once was a colony of Rome. There is a cathedral in Cologne that took seven hundred years to build—the longest time of building in the world.

Another famous city in Germany is Munich. It has one of the most famous opera houses in the world. This opera house was destroyed during World War II but was rebuilt, and operas are given there today. Munich is in the state of Bavaria. This region is famous for its festivals and happy outlook on life.

One interesting festival in Munich is the *Oktoberfest*. Although this is called the October festival, it is actually held in September. It is a carnival and state fair. The most popular attraction at the festival is the famous German beer. Much beer is brewed in Munich. There are over one thousand breweries, most of them small, making thousands of gallons of beer every day. Much of the beer is exported, but during Oktoberfest visitors come from all over the world to have fun and to drink the beer.

The various parts of Germany are different from one another not only in the kind of land in each part but also in the people and their ways of looking at things. In France

below: A village among the trees of the Black Forest

German Tourist Information Office

right: A typical farm house in the Black Forest

---

opposite top: Morning sunlight awakens a Black Forest village

---

opposite bottom: New bridge crosses the Rhine into Cologne

German Tourist Information Office

the people are much alike, but in Germany there are many differences. Cultures differ because Germany has not been a single nation for very long. A group of independent states were united only about a hundred years ago into the country of Germany.

Germany is a rich country in all of the natural resources. You remember that France, Germany's next-door neighbor, is mostly a farming, or agricultural country. Not so Germany. Although Germany is agricultural and has led western and central Europe in the production of many crops such as potatoes, sugar beets, barley, and oats and grows many other things besides, Germany has long been a powerful industrial nation. One of the things that has helped the nation in this field is the huge amount of coal that is deposited in the land. Germany also has water power. Another thing that has made Germany a leader in many industries, particularly in the production of chemicals and synthetics, is its great number of people who are talented in and interested in science.

In the modern world, Germany ranks high among the countries that have produced a special type of manpower— scientists and engineers. Germany also has been a leader in education in western and central Europe.

The country has been a power in foreign trade, and it is no wonder since she is located in the heart of western and central Europe. Germany long acted as the chief supplier of manufactured goods of many kinds to most of Europe.

below right: Peaceful scene on the Rhine River

below left: Castle Stahleck on the banks of the Rhine

East Germany

There have been many boundary changes and divisions of Germany in its rather short, one-hundred-year history.

After World War II, Germany was split into four zones. Then in 1949 the French, English, and U.S. zones became the German Federal Republic. (We call this West Germany.) The Russian zone became a separate country, the German Democratic Republic. (East Germany.) This is a communist country controlled by Russia.

Most of East Germany lies in the plain that extends across northern Europe. Food for dairy cattle is raised along the Baltic Sea. Potatoes, rye, wheat, and sugar beets are the important crops in the central part of the country.

The city of Berlin is in East Germany. Half of the city belongs to West Germany. The shortest distance by car from West Germany to West Berlin is 104 miles. To reach West Berlin, cars and trucks travel along a four-lane concrete highway called an *autobahn*.

The largest city in East Germany, Berlin was the capital of Germany before World War II. Now, a high, guarded wall runs through the city dividing it. Buildings on the borderline have had windows and doors bricked in. One section of the border is the Spree River. The Brandenburg Gate, part of East Germany just inside the border, was built in 1788-91 by King Frederick William II of Prussia. In front of the gate a barbed-wire barricade and armed patrols mark the border.

Berlin was severely damaged by bombs during World War II. But now West Berlin has been rebuilt and it is a large, busy city. New office buildings, apartment houses, and wide avenues have sprung up in West Berlin.

Communist countries do not want people to travel to or from them. It is as if they were separated from the rest of the world by a high fence. Winston Churchill, a great Englishman, called this dividing line an *Iron Curtain*. For this reason we call the countries behind this "fence" Iron Curtain countries.

Switzerland

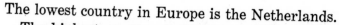

The lowest country in Europe is the Netherlands.

The highest country in Europe is the land of the Swiss people, Switzerland.

There is hardly a hill in the whole of Holland.

Switzerland is nearly all mountains—the highest mountains in western Europe. They are so high that there is snow on them all year, summer and winter. These mighty mountains are the Alps.

Switzerland is not like any other country in all of Europe, in fact in all the world. The people who live there love freedom above everything else. They are famous fighters, too, but they hate war. And they have been able to stay out of the biggest wars because of their location—in the mountains.

But you can't have a mountain without a valley. The mountain tops in Switzerland are white, but the valleys are green, and cows with tinkling bells graze over the fields. The melting snow from the mountain tops makes beautiful waterfalls and bubbling, tinkling brooks in the valleys.

Now it is not easy to get from valley to valley in a region that is all mountains. The only way you can do it is to go through man-made or natural passes. When hopeful conquerors appear, the Swiss people threaten to close the mountain passes if soldiers try to take their land. The invaders go away, because the only thing they really want from Switzerland is the passes. They would make a good route into other countries.

Other people do not want Switzerland itself, because it offers nothing to them. It has very few natural resources. Even agriculture does not provide enough food for the Swiss themselves. They import most of their food.

How do the Swiss make money, then? They make it from industry, but not from big, or heavy, industry. They make their money from the manufacture of many kinds of goods of high quality. Again you see how a small country that cannot manufacture huge quantities of materials relies on quality products for its fame and living. The Swiss are known for making quality products of many kinds, especially watches and clocks, cheese, chocolate, and fine textiles.

The Swiss have had peace for a very long time and yet there are many different types of people in their country. In fact, Switzerland is like many countries in miniature. It does not have a language of its own, but three official languages. They are German, French, and Italian. And there are colonies of German Swiss, French Swiss, and Italian Swiss. These people tend to live in separate parts of Switzerland, but they are all Swiss in heart and loyalty.

Some of the people live in parts of Switzerland that are very dangerous. Have you ever seen the snow on the roof of a house suddenly slide off and fall to the ground? A sudden sliding of snow is called an *avalanche*. But suppose the roof of the house were a mile long, like the side of a mountain. And suppose that suddenly the snow covering it slipped and fell into the valley beneath. That is an avalanche of the kind they have in Switzerland. And sometimes avalanches bury people and houses and even whole villages.

Some long, wide, and high mountain valleys are filled with snow that has turned to ice. The ice filling these long valleys, like a river frozen to the bottom, is called a *glacier*, and the largest of these glaciers have names just as rivers have. There are a thousand glaciers in Switzerland.

Most rivers start from springs, but in Switzerland rivers usually start from melting ice under a glacier. One of these big glaciers in Switzerland is called the Rhône Glacier. From one end of the Rhône Glacier, as from an ice cave, flows a cold stream of melting ice. This stream grows larger and larger as it flows on down the valley and is joined by other streams of melted snow and ice. It is then called the Rhône River. It runs on until it reaches a big, broad valley, which it fills to form a lake—the largest lake in Switzerland, Lake Geneva.

The Rhône flows out again on the other side of Lake Geneva, down through France past Lyons and the mulberry trees and the silkworm farms, and into the Mediterranean Sea.

Another river with the same name as the Rhône, except for one letter, is the Rhine. It, too, starts from beneath a glacier, but the Rhine flows north between France and Germany, through Holland, and into the North Sea.

There are many people in the world who think it great sport to climb mountains—the higher the mountain and

more difficult and the more dangerous it is, the more they like to climb it. The highest mountain in the Alps is Mont Blanc, which means "White Mountain." Part of Mont Blanc is in Switzerland but the top is in France. Every summer many people climb Mont Blanc and other mountains in the Alps.

Probably the hardest of all Swiss mountains to climb is a mountain that looks like a huge horn. It is called the Matterhorn. Only the most skilled and the most daring climbers ever attempt it. From the city of Zermatt, in the valley of the Matterhorn, a cogwheel railroad goes up more than 10,000 feet. From here you can see more than fifty mountain peaks and several glaciers.

In winter, skiing is a very popular sport. People come from all over the world to ski in Switzerland. In Arosa the lake freezes so hard that they have horseraces on the ice. Skiing can be done in the summer, too, on the glaciers but it is dangerous to ski on such icy surfaces.

Many people go to Switzerland to see the beauty of the giant snow-covered mountains, even if they do not climb them. The Swiss have built hotels wherever there is a fine view of a mountain or a waterfall or some other wonderful or beautiful thing to see. There are thousands of such hotels all through the country so that the chief business of the Swiss people seems to be hotel-keeping.

Remember the passes through the mountains in Switzerland? Some of them are very famous. They all have names. One of them is named the Simplon. Napoleon, a French general, once crossed the Simplon Pass with his army into Italy. But you can now go under and through the mountains, for in many places long tunnels have been built.

One of the longest tunnels is St. Gothard. The man who built it started to dig from both sides of the mountain, and the two holes they dug met exactly in the middle. Some people said it was wonderful that two tunnels, each miles long, dug from opposite sides of the mountain, should meet. The men replied, "Not at all. It would have been wonderful

opposite top: Swiss children learning to ski

opposite bottom: Zermatt at the foot of the Matterhorn

if the tunnels hadn't met. We are not moles digging blindly. We had figured it out beforehand and we knew where we were digging."

But the longest tunnel in the world is under the Simplon Pass. At one end of the tunnel is Italy and at the other is Switzerland. This tunnel is over twelve miles long. It takes more than two days to go over the mountain by Simplon Pass, but only sixteen minutes to go through the tunnel!

Near the top of the Simplon Pass is a house called a *hospice*, where you can spend the night. It is a house where certain priests, called monks, live. The reason the hospice was built where it is, and the reason the monks live there, is to provide shelter for travelers and a place where they may rest safely in case they should be caught in a storm.

Few people cross Simplon Pass any more, for it is too dangerous. The tunnel, on the other hand, is safe. Snowstorms and blizzards are likely to happen almost any time, summer or winter, in the pass, and travelers often were lost and frozen to death. The monks living in the hospice were the life-savers of the mountain pass. They had built little huts along the mountain pathway and they had large, strong, intelligent dogs called St. Bernards who were trained to go from the hospice when there was a storm and search for travelers who might have lost their way or fallen in the snow.

In Switzerland there are about 1500 lakes. One of the most beautiful is called the Lake of Light—Lake Lucerne. On the shore of Lake Lucerne is a little church marking the spot where William Tell is supposed to have shot the apple off his young son's head.

About six hundred years ago, Switzerland was not a country, but a group of districts called Cantons. Even then the people were fiercely independent. From time to time, cruel overlords came to the land. One put his hat on a pole in Lucerne and demanded that everyone who passed by must bow to the hat. William Tell refused to do this stupid thing. The overlord said, "He must die. But since he is a great hunter, I may spare his life if he will shoot an apple off his son's head."

opposite: Outdoor William Tell Plays presented in Switzerland

With his bow and arrow, William Tell shot the apple off his son's head, and the crowd cheered.

The overlord asked Tell what he proposed to do with the other arrow in his belt. Tell replied, "If I had killed my son with the first arrow, I would have killed you with this one." This made the overlord furious. Tell was seized by the guards and was being taken in a boat to the prison across the lake when a storm came up. Tell escaped into the mountains. The cruel overlord was killed when he went after his prisoner.

Not long after this—about the time that Columbus was setting off across the sea—the Cantons in the Alps became an independent country, and have been one ever since.

Part of the city of Lucerne is on the Reuss River. Many old buildings still stand on the right bank of the river. Chapel Bridge, one of the six bridges crossing the river, is a wooden-covered medieval bridge. Next to the bridge there is a water tower which was used as a torture chamber in the Middle Ages.

Because Switzerland is a neutral country and does not take part in wars, money standards in Switzerland are steady. Therefore many people from other countries bank and buy insurance in Switzerland. Much banking is done in the city of Basel, which is on the Rhine. Basel is in the northwest corner of Switzerland. If you stand on the bridge over the Rhine on Swiss land, you can see both Germany and France.

above: Geneva, Switzerland on Lake Geneva

Also, because of its neutrality, Swiss embassies often act as mediators, or go-betweens, for two countries who are having a disagreement. The Swiss ambassador will carry or relay messages from one country to the other.

The capital of Switzerland is Bern, also on a river, the Aar. The old section of Bern has medieval arcades, which are like covered sidewalks. You can windowshop in any weather and be protected. The official mascot of Bern is the bear, and in the Bear's Dens visitors can see trained bears performing and entertaining the onlookers.

There are many important universities in Switzerland, and Geneva is the headquarters of many international organizations such as the Red Cross and the International Labor Organization.

At one time Switzerland was a country of small farms and herdsmen. Now only a small group farm, but the cattle on the lovely mountain meadows provide the milk that makes the cheese and chocolate that are important exports.

The fine craftsmanship of the Swiss makes them excel in the arts of wood carving, watch making, furniture painting, and fine embroidery.

The Swiss have used the water power to make electricity. Electric railroads cross valleys and wind around mountains to unite all parts of the country. Breath-taking beauty greets a traveler at every turn.

Switzerland, with its long history of peace, is a nation where people of different national backgrounds, religions, and even different languages, get along well together.

below: The Chapel Bridge and Water Tower in Lucerne
Trans World Airlines Photo

Austria

Look at the map and find Austria. How small it is! Would you ever think that this tiny country was the key to traffic between western and eastern Europe? Well it is and its location makes it so. Six nations border on Austria. They are Germany, Czechoslovakia, Hungary, Yugoslavia, Italy, and Switzerland. So vital is Austria's position that this country once controlled most of these nations. In fact, it was once the center of a huge empire made up of some of these nations. It is still important but it does not control these nations any more.

The capital of Austria is Vienna. For many centuries Vienna was the outpost of Western civilization. What does that mean? It means that it was the city that was farthest removed from the rest of Western civilization but which, nevertheless, was a part of that civilization. It was often fortified against invaders from the east who were not so civilized. Vienna has seen many battles and wars and, in fact, has been right in the middle of them for centuries.

In spite of this fact, modern Vienna is associated with some of the most happy and pleasant things in life—good music and dancing and food and art. The Austrian people have a reputation for being light-hearted, and much of what they have produced has seemed to prove this fact. The world's great waltzes have come from Austria and other great music has come from there. The Blue Danube Waltz tells about the river that runs through the city.

But the Austrians are also great scientists, especially great doctors. In the last century, particularly, Vienna was the center of medical learning for the whole world. The medical school is part of Vienna University, founded in 1365. Many great scientists gather in Vienna for meetings because the permanent headquarters of the International Atomic Energy Commission is here.

From many parts of the city, the delicate spire of St. Stephen's Cathedral can be seen pointing heavenward. This Gothic masterpiece has become the symbol of Vienna.

Austria's most important world role now is once more as an outpost of Western culture and civilization. In the Cold War, Austria sits at the front line, ever watchful. So it continues to be a mighty mite in world affairs.

Austria is something like Switzerland in the character of the land. It is a mountainous country and although it is not quite as rugged as Switzerland, it is more rugged than any of its other neighbors. Austrians carry on both farming and manufacturing to make a living.

The big source of power for manufacturing and other needs is not so much coal as it is water. Austria does have some coal deposits, but its water power is greater and more easily used.

Many years ago, people crossed the Brenner Pass from Italy into Austria. It is said that a road existed across the pass in the year 1000. Now, of course, an autobahn—a modern highway—crosses the pass and comes to a little city called Innsbruck. When travelers first crossed the Alps from Italy, they stopped at this little village on the River Inn. In the Middle Ages, Innsbruck became an important town and capital of the surrounding area. Under Emperor Maximilian I, about 1500, Innsbruck was the Imperial Residence, the place where the court lived.

Today Innsbruck is a modern city with many remains of the past. Once inside the city, a visitor can see that it is surrounded by mountains. Many interesting things remain from the time of Maximilian. A golden roof, a small roof over a window with about 3000 gold-plated tiles glistening on it, can be seen on a building overlooking a square. This window served as a box where royalty could watch entertainment in the square below.

Another charming city in the mountains in Austria is Salzburg. The city is overlooked by the Hohensalzburg Fortress and ruins of fortifications used in the Middle Ages.

Salzburg is the birthplace of a famous composer, Mozart. Music is very important in Salzburg and every year a festival is held. Performances are given in various places throughout the city. People come from all over to attend this renowned festival. The whole city becomes the stage for opera, serenades, and church music.

right: Looking down on Salzburg

Northern Europe

Norway, Sweden, Denmark, and Finland—countries we call Scandinavian—have many things in common. The sea affects life in all of them. They have similar languages. The land is rugged. The action of glaciers, especially in Norway, carved out river valleys that were flooded by the sea. These narrow inlets with their high rocky walls are called *fiords*. The people of these countries have made the most of their rather thin natural resources. Many of them farm in the summer and fish for cod in the winter. They use their water power in producing wood products from their forest lands. The forests are important in Finland, for almost half of this country is wasteland where very little grows.

You might expect the water in the fiords of Norway to be cold, because the country is so far north. But the warmth brought by the Gulf Stream keeps the fiords from freezing. This river in the sea that picks up its warmth from the sun in the Gulf of Mexico seems to end at the most northern city in the world. This is Hammerfest, Norway. The Gulf Stream dumps wood on the shore that may have come all the way from the Gulf of Mexico. People gather this driftwood and use it for fires. Ordinary wood burns with a yellow flame. But wood that is filled with minerals from the sea burns with blue, green, and purple flames.

Norwegian fishermen go to islands called the Lofodens to catch cod. Oil from the cod livers is bottled and sold and the flesh of the cod is dried for market.

The city of Bergen on the Bergen Fiord is called the fishiest city in the world. Fishermen bring boatloads of cod to Bergen. From the Lofoden Islands and the fiords they bring their catches—little fish, big fish, thick fish, thin fish.

Bergen is also the wettest city in Europe. People carry umbrellas or raincoats all the time. When it is not raining, it seems to be getting ready to rain. It takes a lot of rain to make an inch of rain, if you catch it in a bucket. Bergen has a rainfall of six feet in a year!

Pan American World Airlines

above: A stave church in Norway

Norwegian American Lines

below: The Fostedal Glacier in Norway

Bob Brunton—Hollis Associates

Photo by John P. Reidy

above: English Coat of Arms

---

right: Horse guards leave
their post after
sentry duty, London, England

left: A small country
village in Portugal

---

below: The matador,
dressed in rich clothes,
enters the arena for
the bullfight in Spain

---

right: A kiosk
along the Seine River
advertises
coming events, Paris

Photo by John P. Reidy

Photo by Berenice O'Connor

above: In Capri,
an island off Italy in the
Mediterranean Sea,
men relax and talk in
the warm sun

---

left: Along the Amalfi Drive
in Italy, towns come down the
steep sides to the
Mediterranean Sea

71

The white marble
Parthenon crowns
the Acropolis
overlooking
Athens, Greece

Deep in the Black Forest
the father of
ski champion Albert Toma
teaches children to ski.
Hinterzarten, Germany

74

Swiss flag flies on a
resort hotel in the
snow-covered Alps

right: Ornate onion
domes of
St. Basil's Church

below left: Glassblower
in Kosta, Sweden

below right: In Copenhagen,
Denmark, children amuse
themselves in Tivoli
Gardens, the world's
most famous
amusement park

Alpha Photo Associates Inc.

Photo by Chan Forman

Photo by Chan Forman

Photo by Chan Forman

The city of Bergen,
Norway, seems
to be built into
the forested hills

Norwegians have always been famous seamen. Long, long ago these northland sailors were called "Vikings." This, however, does not mean Vi-kings, but Vik-ings, which means "fiordmen." They were sailing across the Atlantic five hundred years before Columbus.

Later Scandinavian explorers—Nansen and Amundsen —tried to reach the North Pole. They did not succeed, although Amundsen did find the South Pole. He was the first to reach it.

Mountain tops of Norway and Sweden have great fields of ice and snow. As this ice and snow sinks toward the valleys, it melts. The water falls in streams like rain running off a roof in a water spout. This falling water is used in Norway and Sweden to turn wheels. The turning wheels run sawmills and machinery, just as wheels are turned by steam that is made by heating water with coal. The people of Norway and Sweden call their waterfalls "white coal."

White coal cannot do one thing that black coal can do. It will not heat. In northern Sweden there are iron mines. This iron is particularly good for making tools that have sharp edges like knives and razors. But there is no coal to melt the iron out of the ore. So a lot of the iron ore is shipped to England where there is plenty of coal. There, the English make fine cutlery. Now Sweden makes its own steel, but has to import coal to do it.

Have you ever seen a picture of pine trees in the snow, or all covered with snow? Pine trees like this cover much of Norway, Sweden, and Finland. These pines make good masts for ships. They make flagpoles and telephone poles. They provide lumber for building. They even make fine match sticks, and millions of match sticks can be made from a single tree. If you look on a box of wooden matches, you may see "Made in Sweden" stamped on the box.

Small trees are ground into pulp, which is used to make paper. The forests of Scandinavian countries are used wisely and in many ways.

opposite top: Winter scene in Norway

opposite, bottom left: Spring blooms in Sweden

opposite, bottom right: Timber on the River Dalälvan, Sweden

Royal Consulate General of Sweden, Chicago

Royal Consulate General of Sweden, Chicago

North Cape, at the top of Norway, juts out into the Arctic Ocean. There is no town there, but people make long trips from other lands to North Cape to see the sun shining on the sea in the middle of the night. At North Cape it is night for six months and day for six months. During the winter months the sun does not rise above the horizon. During the summer months the sun does not set. It seems to circle the horizon. This is why you can see the sun shining on the sea in the middle of the night.

Sweden and Norway used to be one country with one king ruling over it. Now they are separate countries and each has a king of its own, and a capital city.

Lapland is a section of land in the northern part of Europe extending across Norway, Sweden, Finland, and Russia. More than half of this land is inside the arctic circle so the weather is cold the year round. Many minerals

Consulate General of Finland

and great forests are found here. Many of the Lapps raise large herds of reindeer and the meat, skins, and horns are used in trade.

Denmark is the storybook land, home of Hans Christian Andersen and the *Ugly Duckling* and other stories that have been enjoyed for over two hundred years.

Denmark, except for forty-two miles of border along Germany, is completely surrounded by water. In some towns almost every person is either a sailor, a ship-builder, or connected with shipping in some way.

Most of the Danes who stay at home are engaged in dairy farming. They raise cows for milk to make butter, and they raise chickens for eggs. Danish butter and eggs are sent to other countries.

There are two chief parts of Denmark. One is a thumb-like peninsula called Jutland. The other is a little island right alongside Jutland called Zealand. Zealand means "Sea Land." It is an island, and Copenhagen, the capital, is here.

Copenhagen means "Merchant's Harbor." Merchants used to stop there on the way from the North Sea to the Baltic. But there are not so many ships now as there once were. Instead of going around Jutland to get from the North Sea to the Baltic Sea, ships take a short cut through the Kiel Canal. The Germans built this canal across the base of the thumb of Jutland to give them easy access to the North Sea.

Denmark once owned Iceland and still owns Greenland. There are Eskimos in Greenland, a cold country where vegetables are grown under glass. There are millions of birds called *auks* in Greenland. Eskimos use the soft feathers of the auks to line their clothes to keep them warm, for it gets very cold in Greenland. Eskimos hunt the

opposite: Transportation of the Finnish Lapps

right: A Lapp mother with her child, Sweden

83

musk-ox and the walrus for food. Walrus tusks are valuable, too. Thule is a walrus and polar-bear hunting center in Greenland. Many pure Eskimos live in this settlement.

As in Lapland, reindeer herds are kept in Greenland. Dogsleds are used for transportation in many of the frozen areas. Seals are hunted too. The hunters hide behind white screens and shoot through a hole in the screen to catch a seal. Many of the Eskimos use the seal meat for food and the skins are sold to use in making coats.

The only tame animals the Eskimo has are the Eskimo dogs that pull his sleds.

Mining is also done in Greenland where there are lead-zinc mines and coal.

Iceland is a rocky island west of Norway. The center of this small republic is a high plateau ringed by mountains. One volcanic mountain was active in 1947 and some of the land is covered with lava. There are hot springs here and geysers shoot streams of hot water and steam into the air. There are farmlands along the sheltered southwest coast, and several good harbors. Short, swift rivers provide water power for the industries of Iceland.

below: Hunting seal

_____

opposite top: Fishing vessel in
a Greenland fiord

_____

opposite bottom: Eskimos with
their kayak

Danish Information Office

Southern Europe

Spain, Portugal, Italy and Greece. Whenever you read about ancient history or about the history of the times when the New World was being discovered and settled, you hear about these countries. They have been very important to the development of Western civilization. In fact, at various times in the history of the world, these were the leading nations, the big powers in world affairs.

None of these nations are big powers any longer. They have come into hard times, and they are among the least progressive countries in the modern world. That is surprising isn't it? But there are reasons for this. We know that the people who live in southern Europe have always been among the smartest and most daring people in the whole world. How is it then that they are not doing so well in the modern world? As you might expect from the things you have learned in this book, part of the trouble comes from their location, what the land has to offer them, and what it does not have to offer them.

As you know from your maps, the people in southern Europe are cut off from the rest of the continent by mountains. But what you may not know is that the land there, at least most of it, is rugged. Most of it is made up of highlands. Highlands include plateaus, hills, and mountains. The lowlands are mostly near the coastal parts. In Spain there is a high plateau like a mountain with its top smoothed down. Italy has more than its share of high mountains including the Italian Alps and the Apennines. There are many mountains in Greece, too. These highlands give the people a certain amount of protection from invasion, but they are also hard to work.

Climate generally is not a friend in many ways either. Because of the mountains that stretch across southern Europe from east to west, the Arctic winds get cut off, so there are no severe winters in southern Europe. That sounds good, doesn't it? But if the cold from the north has to stop at the mountains, the heat from the south has to stop there, too. Southern Europe has a subtropical climate because of these things. In fact, it has the warmest summers in all of Europe.

A subtropical climate is good if there is enough rain to go with the warmth. But here southern Europe is not lucky. It

below: The island of Samos, Greece

does not really have enough rain in all parts. Most of the plants are stunted or gnarled or scrubby. Certain things do grow well, but these are different from the things that grow in the rest of Europe. In southern Europe the trees that grow best are cork oak, olive, cypress, and cedar. They are certainly different from the big hardy pines that grow in northern Europe. The trees that grow in southern Europe do not yield many forest products in comparison with those that are produced in the rest of Europe. The main food crops in southern Europe are wheat, barley, beans, chick-peas, and lentils.

Because the temperatures are high, oranges, lemons, rice, and many vegetables can be grown. But to grow these crops, many farmers have to irrigate the land. One does not usually think of irrigating land in Europe, but in southern Europe it is important. Grapes of certain types do well in southern Europe, too.

The crops that are grown in a country usually affect the kind of cooking the people do. Southern Europeans use olive oil as the fat for cooking. That is not surprising, since they produce olives. And many southern European dishes call for rice. They grow that, too. Peas are in their favorite foods, and they also are grown in the area.

Cattle and hogs do not do very well in the kind of climate that southern Europe has, but goats, sheep, mules, and donkeys do. So these are the animals that are most often seen in that region. You probably already know that lamb is among the most popular meats of the people from southern Europe. Now you can see why this is so.

Southern Europe has a lot of different minerals but not a lot of any one kind. Long, long ago, these minerals were enough for the people who lived there. But in the modern world they are not. The area also has too little coal, petroleum, and iron. Now remember that we live in an "alloy age." Many very important products that we use are made of steel, which is made from iron and other things, and which needs coal or some other fuel in its making.

opposite: Little girl on her way to school in southern Italy

There is manufacturing in southern Europe, but only a very small part of the population there makes a living that way.

Some people in southern Europe are very wealthy, of course, but most of the people are not. Do you remember that we said the people of northern Europe live especially well considering the size and limited resources of the area? Well, just the opposite is true for most of the people of southern Europe.

Spain and Portugal

The people in Spain and Portugal work mostly in agriculture. Only about one-third of the land can be farmed. The other two-thirds is either wasteland or good only for grazing. The people who live here need imagination to make the most of what they have. At one time they claimed a lot of land in other places in the world. In fact, all of Latin America once belonged to one or the other of these countries. But now their world holdings are very small.

Spain once owned a lot of Europe, too. But now she doesn't even own all of Spain! On the map Spain seems to be rubbing noses with a part of Africa. This nose of Spain is called Gibraltar, but Gibraltar does not belong to Spain. It belongs to England.

Gibraltar looks like a nose on the map, but if you were in a boat out on the Mediterranean Sea, Gibraltar would look like a long, high rock. Between it and Africa there is a narrow strip of water called the Strait of Gibraltar. It is only about thirteen miles across. Powerful currents pull and push in and out from the Atlantic Ocean, and only recently has anyone been able to swim across it. Inside the Rock of Gibraltar, England has cut hallways and rooms and windows with long-distance guns in them, and placed her soldiers there to watch out over the water. In time of war, the soldiers can fire on ships that England wants to keep from passing through the water-gate.

Long years ago most of the known world was around the edge of the Mediterranean Sea. Sailors at that time thought it dangerous to go outside this gate called the Strait of Gibraltar and into the great ocean. As the story goes, they set up pillars on each side of the strait like gateposts. They called them the Pillars of Hercules, and put up a sign to warn sailors that it was dangerous to go beyond them. The sign said "Non Plus Ultra," which means "nothing more beyond."

It was supposed that not far outside the Pillars of Hercules the ocean came to an edge where ships would tumble off to a bottomless nothing. Columbus did not believe any such thing. He was not afraid. He sailed from Spain starting from a place outside the Pillars of Hercules called Palos. He sailed on until, as you know, he came to America.

Just before Columbus sailed from Spain there were people living there called Moors, who had come across from Africa and made their home there. The Moors were different from other people in Europe. They were not Christians. They believed in Mohammed and a god whom they called Allah. The Moors built beautiful palaces, but they were different from European palaces. The Moorish princes lived in one of these palaces on a hill in the city of Granada, which is not far from Gibraltar. The palace in Granada was called the Alhambra.

below: Old section of Granada, Spain

Spanish National Tourist Office

The Christians in Spain did not like the Moors, so they fought with them until they drove the Moors out of Spain back into Africa. The Spanish queen received Columbus in the Alhambra and said goodbye to him there before he sailed for the New World. No one lives in the Alhambra now, but it is still on the hill at Granada, and Spain keeps it as it once was so that people may visit it.

The walls of the Alhambra are covered with beautiful colored tiles. The doorways are shaped like horseshoes and the courtyards have splashing fountains and walled-in pools where the Moorish princesses used to bathe.

A city in Spain called Seville has a great cathedral, the second-largest church in the world. It was built after the Moors had been driven out of Spain. The spot on which it stands was the spot where a Moorish church once stood. In

below: A peasant in his haywagon in Segovia, Spain. A turreted castle stands in the background

this cathedral are buried what are supposed to be the ashes of Columbus.

Almost every city and town in Spain has a bullring, because bullfighting is the national sport of Spain, just as it is of some Latin American countries. A bullfighter has to be brave and skillful, for if his foot slipped on the sandy ground he might not be able to avoid the bull's horns, and could be killed. Since bullfighting is the national sport, for the boys in Spain playing bullfighting is a favorite game. One boy acts as the bull and another as the fighter.

The girls in Spain do not play at bullfighting, but at dancing. Spain is famous for its dances and its dancers. It seems as if everyone in Spain is a good dancer. People even dance in front of the altar in churches as a way of glorifying God, just as they sing in church for the same purpose.

Spanish houses have no front yard nor back nor side yard, but an inside yard with the rooms all around it. This inside yard is called a *patio* and is often a living room and dining room for all who live in the house.

As you ride through Spain or Portugal on a train you can see a very peculiar looking tree. It is the cork tree we mentioned earlier. The corks we use for bottle stoppers don't grow on trees as cherries do. They are made from the bark of the cork oak. The bark is cut from the tree in large pieces and these, in turn, are cut up into corks of different sizes. The tree then grows another coat of bark, but it takes nine years to grow bark thick enough to be cut again.

Cork trees live to a great age, much longer than people do. But another tree you see in Spain and Portugal grows to be still older. It is the olive tree. Olive trees have been known to live and bear fruit for a thousand years! Spaniards and other people of southern Europe grow olive trees for their fruit. They eat them as they are but they also grow them for their oil. We told you before that people in southern Europe use olive oil as their main cooking fat. They also make very fine soap from it. This soap is called Castile soap.

Madrid is the capital of Spain, and claims to be much like Paris. Madrid is near the center of the country. Old Madrid had narrow streets and small houses. New Madrid has broad boulevards and big buildings and if you did not hear the people speaking Spanish, you might think you were in Paris or New York or some other large and important city of the world.

right: A Spanish lady
sewing in the street

opposite: Alcala-Jose Antonia
Street, Madrid's main street

In old Spain men always said *mañana* (mahn-yahn'ah), which means "tomorrow," for they put off everything they could "until tomorrow." New Spain says "do it now."

The capital of Portugal, Lisbon, is a seaport built on hills overlooking the natural harbor. Many explorers sailed from this port in the great time of discovery. The Jeronimos Cathedral, at the edge of the city, was built to commemorate the successful voyage of Vasco da Gama, who sailed around the tip of Africa and reached India in 1497. His tomb is inside the cathedral.

opposite: Jeronimos Cathedral in Lisbon, Portugal

Italy

Italy played such an important part in the history of the ancient world and also in the history of the world at the time of the Renaissance, that people come from all over the world to visit it and to see firsthand the places they have read about. Tourism is a big business in Italy these days—one of the country's most important.

You have heard of the "old woman who lived in a shoe, who had so many children she didn't know what to do." On the map, Italy looks like a shoe, or at least like a boot, and in it live more men, women, and children than the country seems able to support. A lot of Italian people have gone elsewhere in the world, especially to the United States.

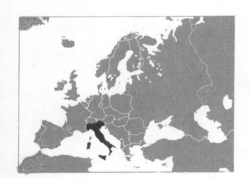

The large industrial cities of Italy are in the north. Milan is now a modern city where the skyscrapers make the large cathedral seem very small.

Turin is another large northern city. In these cities, sewing machines, automobiles, and many other things are made for Italy and also for other countries all over the world. Many people from the poor southern sections come to the north to find employment in the large factories.

The very first Italian to come to the New World was, of course, Christopher Columbus. He went to the New World for Spain, but he was an Italian by birth. He was born in the city of Genoa. A part of his house is still standing in Genoa, and there is a statue of him just outside the railroad station there. Ships still sail from Genoa to the United States.

On the other side of the boot top from Genoa is another city that is not *near* water but is *in*-water. It is built on many little islands, and the streets are water with bridges across them. This city is called Venice. The water streets are called *canals*, and the main street, which would be a broad avenue if it were paved is called the Grand Canal. The Grand Canal is 200 feet wide. Altogether there are 150 canals in Venice and 400 bridges. Public transportation is provided by motor boats that stop at piers. The passengers get on and pay their fare and ride to the stop they want.

Instead of automobiles the people ride boats up and down the water streets. These boats are painted black and in the center there is a little cabin. These boats are called *gondolas* and a man called a *gondolier* stands back of the little cabin and rows the gondola with one long oar.

Long ago people built beautiful palaces along the canals. You can still see them today. Another famous building in Venice is a church called St. Mark's. It has five domes, one on each corner and one big one in the center, but these domes are not like those of St. Paul's in London. They are shaped like an onion.

Inside St. Mark's and outside too, are hundreds of pictures made with bits of colored stone and gold and colored glass. Such pictures are called *mosaics*. They do not fade or peel off or wash off as painted pictures do.

The largest piece of land in Venice is the paved square in front of St. Mark's. In this square there are flocks of pigeons so tame they will alight on your hand or shoulder to be fed. At one time long ago Venice was saved from an enemy by a message brought by a carrier pigeon. Ever since then people who live in Venice have treated pigeons very well. Anyone who harms a pigeon will be arrested and punished.

Venice is now a city in the country of Italy, but it used to be a little country itself. It made its own money and had its own ruler who was called a Doge (dozhe), which means "Duke." A Doge ruled and lived in a palace. He also punished people who had done wrong. Just across the canal from the Doge's palace was a prison, and connecting the palace with the prison was a covered bridge. When a man was sent to prison by the Doge, he crossed over this bridge, sighing and groaning. So this bridge came to be called the "Bridge of Sighs."

The Venetians made their living in the first place out of two common things right at hand. They were salt and fish. There was also a lot of another common thing right at hand. This was sand. Sand does not seem to have much value, but the Venetians found that they could make glass out of sand my melting it in a furnace with something else. They found out, too, that they could blow this melted glass as one blows soap bubbles, and that by blowing it in this

right: The Bridge of Sighs, Venice

opposite: Aerial view of
St. Mark's Cathedral and Square

---

left: Glass blowing in Murano,
Venice, Italy

way they could make different shapes from it. Venice became famous for its glass vases, bowls, drinking glasses, and figures of animals and other things.

Down the length of Italy like the back of a sea monster is a ridge of mountains called the Apennines (ahp'ah-nynz). Across the Apennine Mountains there is another famous city called Florence. As the train comes into Florence, it curves around the city. You see above the housetops near the center of the city a large dome that looks like the hub of a wheel about which the train is turning. Next to the dome is a big square tower. Both the tower and the dome were built before Columbus was born. The dome looks like the dome of St. Paul's in London. To be correct, you should say that the dome of St. Paul's looks like the dome of the Cathedral of Florence, because the dome of St. Paul's and dome of the Capitol building in the United States and a lot of other domes were copied from the one in Florence.

A dome like this is hard to build, but the people in Florence figured out how to do it. You see, the dome is built of pieces of stone and the stones have to cover a space beneath without falling, just as the stones in a bridge or an arch must do. No cement is strong enough to hold stones together so that they will not fall when placed across an open space, but if the stones can be held up by some wooden framework until every stone is in place, then the wooden framework underneath can be taken away and the stone will not fall. Why? Well all the stones in a curving arch will push downward at the same time and as all push downward together they get wedged in so tightly that none can fall.

Florence was a city that wanted beautiful things. Some of Italy's finest artists have come from Florence and have worked in Florence. One of them was Michelangelo. One of his most beautiful sculptures, a figure of the Biblical David, is in Florence.

Florence is on the Arno River. The city's oldest bridge crossing the river is the Ponte Vecchio which means "old bridge." All along the bridge are shops selling silver, leather goods, cloth, and straw articles.

right: The Ponte Vecchio with its many shops, Florence

Not very far from Florence is the city of Pisa where there is a famous tower. It is not famous because it is beautiful or big or anything like that. It is famous because it leans to one side. It is called the Leaning Tower of Pisa. The tower was built to stand straight, but the foundation has sunk on one side so that the tower slants over and looks as if it were going to fall. It has stood that way for hundreds of years, but is gradually leaning more and more. If it cannot be stopped, someday it will fall.

Pisa is famous for something else, too. Near Pisa are stone mines called quarries that have some of the finest marble in the world. It is called Carrara marble after the name of the place where it is found. Carrara marble is in demand for beautiful sculptures and fine ornaments.

below: Beautiful marble is taken from the hills around Carrara

Rome is the capital of Italy. Rome was once the capital of the ancient Roman Empire. Rome is also the capital of the Roman Catholic Church, for here is where the Pope lives, and he is the head of that church. He lives in a section of Rome called the Vatican, which is like a city inside a city. The Vatican has its own government and belongs only to itself even though it is in Rome.

It is here that St. Peter's Church is. St. Peter's is one of the most famous churches in the whole world because it is so beautiful. Some of the world's greatest artists helped to build it. Among them was Michelangelo, who painted beautiful pictures on the ceiling of part of it.

The Pope lives next door to St. Peter's in the Vatican, which has more than a thousand rooms, many of which are

below: A quiet time in St. Peter's Square

filled with beautiful works of art. These rooms are museums that people can visit.

Before the time of St. Peter, when people believed in many gods, another church was built in Rome "To All the Gods." This building is still standing. It is called the Pantheon.

Most of the buildings in Rome that were built about the time of Christ are in ruins, but the Pantheon is still almost the same as it was when it was first built. One of the most famous ruins in the world is the Forum, which was a great marketplace of ancient Rome. Around the Forum were beautiful palaces, courthouses, temples, and arches. The arches were built so that victorious generals returning from the wars might ride in triumph through them. One of these arches is called the Arch of Titus. Another is the Arch of Constantine.

Part of the Colosseum is also still standing. That was the enormous arena where the Romans held their sporting events. Looking closely at the Colosseum, you can see the holes where marble used to be attached to the walls. The marble was used to decorate other buildings in Rome.

There are many squares or circles in Rome, called *piazzas*. In these piazzas and tucked into little corners are fountains with flowing water and wonderful works of sculpture.

below: The Bay of Naples

Sabena Belgian World Airlines

above: Mt. Vesuvius from the Bay of Naples

The ruins found throughout the city are of interest to many people. When new buildings are being built, sometimes workmen come across buried treasures. All ruins found during building must be reported to the authorities, but sometimes the contractor isn't very happy to report that he has found some ruins. This is because, if the ruins are important, work on the building may be stopped for a long time.

In the modern train station, on the lower floor, is a ruin that was found during construction. This was just left there and the work completed.

A pile of ashes is not usually very beautiful, but in Italy there is a pile of ashes that everyone thinks is beautiful. It is nearly a mile high and is in the back yard of a city called

Naples, on the beautiful Bay of Naples. People have built their homes and hotels around the bay so they can have a view of Mount Vesuvius. This pile of ashes is called Mount Vesuvius, though it's not really a mountain at all.

Legend says that a lame blacksmith lives down under the ground and that he keeps a huge furnace buring there to heat the iron with which he works. His name, they said, was Vulcan. When they saw smoke coming from a mountain they said it was from Vulcan's forge. We know that this is not true. We know such mountains are volcanoes. One of the best-known volcanoes in the world is Vesuvius.

A long time ago people built their houses very near Vesuvius in a place called Pompeii. Then the volcano erupted and covered the whole city and the people in it with hot *lava*. For a long time Pompeii lay buried. Then one day, hundreds of years later, people dug it out. They found the whole city just as it had been when Vesuvius erupted. It told us a lot about life in the early Roman times. It is now a famous tourist place.

Sicily is an island at the tip of the boot of Italy and is part of Italy. On Sicily is a volcano that is the highest active volcano in Europe. The name of this volcano is Mount Etna and it erupts very often. The lava cools and it is used in construction in the area around the volcano.

right: Characteristic view of the city of Naples

Italian State Tourist Office—ENIT

Greece

Greece is a mountainous land. The two parts of the mainland, like North and South America, are joined by a narrow neck of land called the Isthmus of Corinth.

The countless rocky islands of Greece are the tops of old mountains, now surrounded by water. They are beautiful islands set in the sparkling Aegean Sea. But some of them have very little soil and some have no fresh water. Fresh water has to be brought by boat from a neighboring island. These islands are popular resort areas. Mykonos and Siphnos capture the visitor with their charming whitewashed buildings and easy way of life.

Greece, like Italy, is famous for its past glories. People travel thousands of miles to see the places in Greece that history has made famous, just as they do to see famous places in Italy.

Greece is very small, but even so, it was at one time the greatest country in the world, its people were the greatest people, and its language was the greatest language in the world. At a time when the rest of the people in Europe were fairly uncivilized, the people in Greece were writing great books, building beautiful buildings, making beautiful statues, and teaching in excellent schools.

In the northern part of Greece was the great city of Athens, which is today the capital of modern Greece. Here you can see ruins of the ancient Greek buildings on the hill called the Acropolis. The most beautiful of these buildings is the Parthenon, the temple built to honor the goddess Athena. This ancient building overlooks the modern city of Athens.

Greece today is famous not for her poetry or sculpture or beautiful buildings. It is famous for currants, the little dried grapes that are used in cakes and puddings. Currants are named for Corinth, the stem that joins northern and southern Greece. Greece is also well known for its tobacco, which Greek farmers produce in greater amounts than any other crop except the cereals. Some people think that Greek tobacco is the best in the world.

Greece is becoming more and more famous for its textiles. These are produced mainly in small factories, but some textiles are hand woven. Most of the materials for weaving are imported cotton and wool. There are many skilled craftsmen in Greece, so the people rely on quality rather than on quantity of material. You see again how the small countries with limited resources make quality products to sell in the world market.

Even though Greece is mainly an agricultural country, she cannot raise enough food for her own people, and must import food. Trade with other nations is very important to Greece.

opposite: The Greek island
of Mykonos

below: Athens from the Acropolis

Trans World Airlines Photo

Eastern Europe

Between Russia and the rest of Europe are seven countries that make up eastern Europe. All of them are Communist countries like Russia. Because there was a time when none of these countries would allow people from other places to visit them, they came to be called Iron Curtain countries. These countries were most isolated from the rest of the world just after World War II, which is when they became Communist countries. Later, these countries did let people visit them. In fact, they began to encourage tourists to come to them. Tourism brings money into a country and these countries need the money that tourism brings.

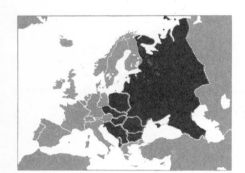

The seven countries of eastern Europe are Poland, Czechoslovakia (Chek-uh-slow-vahk'ee-ah), Hungary, Romania, Bulgaria, Yugoslavia, and Albania. (The western part of Russia is also in Europe.) These countries have often been referred to as the "Shatter Belt," because through the years the land that belongs to them has so often been split up into other countries. The people who live there have often called the area the "Devil's Belt," because the countries in it have no good natural defenses to help the people protect themselves from invaders.

Eastern Europe has always played an especially important part in the affairs of the continent. She acts as a barrier between European countries and the giant country of Russia. That is still its major importance to Europe.

These countries used to be important to Europe in another way, too. Here was produced much of Europe's food. Most of these countries for hundreds of years have produced more food than they needed. They used to sell foodstuffs to the rest of Europe in return for manufactured goods. Eastern Europe is no longer important in this way, however, for ever since World War II, when these coun-

opposite top: One of the many forests in Poland

opposite bottom: Harvesting time in Bulgaria

tries became satellites of Russia, the extra food they produce has been sold to Russia. The people in return obtain manufactured goods from Russia. They do very little business with other countries except for special items.

The fact that eastern Europe produces a lot of extra food tells us much about its climate and its land. We know that for the most part the land can be farmed and that mountains are not much of a problem. We also know that the region gets enough, but not too much, rain. We could guess that even though the winters might be cold, the summers must be hot and long enough for crops to mature. All of these things are so.

There has always been industry in Poland and in Czechoslovakia. Since World War II, the people in eastern Europe have been developing more industry. Their economy, the production and distribution of goods, is planned in the Russian way. It is controlled by their governments. That is not so in other parts of Europe or in North America or in South America either. But it is always true in Communist countries.

Most of the people in eastern Europe live fifty miles from the seas, where it is humid. They are not great fishermen or shipbuilders because the sea is not an important part of their lives as it is in the lives of the Danes, Greeks, Norwegians, Englishmen, and some others in Europe.

You might think that everyone in eastern Europe has always had plenty to eat since agriculture is so important to them and they produce extra food. But that is not the case. Their food consumption is low and always has been, because they need to sell as much of it as possible in order to get other things, like manufactured products. So you see the people of eastern Europe have never been rich as a group.

Poland, which means "flat land," is almost as large as Finland. Poland has much farmland, of course, and iron and coal mines as well. That is why it has been an industrial as well as an agricultural country for a long time. One thing that always has been very important to the people of Poland is music. Chopin (show'pan), one of the world's greatest composers, was Polish.

opposite: Prague Castle in Czechoslovakia

During World War II, a concentration camp system was located in and around Auschwitz. Many, many people, mostly Jews, were killed in these camps. One camp, Cracow, is a museum. The invasion of Poland by the Germans in 1939 began World War II. Poland was quickly crushed and was occupied all during the war. Now it is controlled by the U.S.S.R.

Warsaw, the capital, was almost completely destroyed during the war, but many buildings have been restored and new ones have been built.

Czechoslovakia has long been famous for its manufactured goods. China dishes and glassware are among the important products. There is some heavy industry as well.

Hungary was named for the Huns, who lived in the land long ago. In Hungary today there are many kinds of people.

Two especially interesting groups are the Magyars (mag'yahrz), who are descended from the Chinese, and the Gypsies. Hungary was once part of the huge Austro-Hungarian Empire. At that time Austria and Hungary were one country. The Danube River, which flows through this area, was nearly as famous for castles as the Rhine.

Though there are Gypsies in Hungary, most of the Gypsies in eastern Europe live in Romania. The language of Romania is very different from the languages of the other eastern European countries. The Romanian language is a *Romance* language, which means that it came originally from the old Roman language, Latin. Other Romance languages are French, Italian, Portuguese, and Spanish.

Bulgaria is the country next to the Black Sea. In this country there are forests and mountains as well as farm-

below: A view of Romania from the Carpathian Mountains

Romanian Embassy

116

lands. Bears, wildcats, and wild boars live in the forests. The ibex, a kind of wild goat, lives there too. A goatlike antelope called a chamois (shammy) lives in the mountains. We get the name for chamois, or "shammy," cloths, used for washing automobiles, from this animal. At one time chamois cloths actually were made of the soft leather from the skin of the chamois, but now they are made from other materials, too.

An important business of the Bulgarians is perfume making. They raise fields of roses from which they make a very fine and expensive perfume called attar of roses. It takes a whole roomful of rose petals to make one tiny bottle of attar of roses.

Grapes are grown for wine, and tobacco is exported. The largest city, and the capital, is Sofia, which was settled more than 2000 years ago.

below: Picturesque houses in Sinaia, Romania

Romanian Embassy

Albania is a small country where most of the people raise farm crops or cattle and sheep. In parts of Albania many men and boys wear a white cap that is shaped something like a Turkish fez.

The country of Yugoslavia is just across the Adriatic Sea from Italy. It has many forests. It also has copper mines. Coastal cities on the Adriatic Sea are set on hillsides. This is a popular vacation area. The mountains drop off to the sea and the sea cuts into the land making coves and harbors that provide places for boats. In the mountains, hunting is a popular activity, for there are many different kinds of animals—bear, deer, chamois, wild boar, hare, pheasant, partridge, and duck. Many people ski in the winter.

Skopje (skahp'yay), a city in the southern section of Yugoslavia, had a terrible earthquake in 1963. Many of the buildings were destroyed and many people were injured or killed. New buildings are being built and the city is once more alive, thanks to the help of many countries.

opposite top: Panorama of Zagreb, Yugoslavia

opposite bottom: St. Stefen, Yugoslavia, on the Mediterranean

Russia

Most of the large important cities of Russia are in the European section, or the western section, of the country.

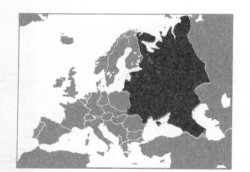

The principal port on the Black Sea and the second largest city is Leningrad. Peter the Great of Russia built Leningrad in 1703 and named it St. Petersburg. This city with its large stone buildings was the capital of Russia until 1918.

Now the capital of Russia is Moscow. The Kremlin is a city within a city. Inside this walled city are churches and cathedrals, palaces and museums, and residential and office buildings. One side of the Kremlin faces Red Square, which is a large open area. At one end of Red Square is St. Basil's Church. This interesting-looking building with its onion-shaped domes is now a museum.

The subway stations in Moscow are world famous for their beautiful design.

Some small countries on the Black Sea were taken as part of Russia during World War II. Some of these countries do not want to be governed by or belong to Russia. One country trying to free itself from Russian domination is Lithuania. This little agricultural land has a history of domination.

opposite: The Kremlin at night, Moscow

KLM Royal Dutch Airlines

The Storybook Lands of Europe

There are some lands in Europe that are either independent or partly dependent on other countries. They are like small storybook lands. These are Liechtenstein (lick'ten-stine), Monaco (mahn'uh-ko), Andorra (an-dore'uh), and San Marino (san mah-ree'no). These lands are not really very important in the affairs of the world, or even in the affairs of Europe, but they are wonderful places for tourists to go.

Monaco is on the Mediterranean coast at the south of France, and it is loosely attached to France politically. It is a tiny place that has no taxes, and no real trade, either. Monaco makes money by running a large gambling casino, the most famous one in the whole world. It is called Monte Carlo. The citizens of Monaco do not usually gamble there. People from all over the world come there to gamble. Monaco makes money from this gambling and uses it to run the country.

Prince Ranier is the head of Monaco. On a trip to the United States he met a beautiful Hollywood movie star named Grace Kelly. He married her, and the movie star became a princess and went to live in Monaco.

Andorra is another land that is closely tied to France. It is in the mountains between France and Spain. Andorra is ruled by the President of France and a Roman Catholic Bishop. What makes Andorra so interesting to many people is the legend of how it came into being. We are not sure how true it is, but the legend says that Charlemagne gave the people of Andorra a charter that created their land. He did this, the legend says, because the Andorran people had helped him in fighting the Moors. That was very long ago, of course.

The Andorrans don't have a gambling casino to make money. They make money by farming or as shepherds. Tourism is also important.

San Marino is the oldest republic in the whole world. It is a landlocked country surrounded by Italy. San Marino was one of the independent Italian states in the old Roman days, and is the only one left. Most of the country is a mountain with three peaks. On one mountain peak is a castle and on the other two are towers.

San Marino governs itself by electing members to councils. Italy does not take part in the government. Most of the people who live in San Marino are farmers who raise crops or livestock. Money is also made from the sale of postage stamps, particularly to stamp collectors. Tourists are important here just as they are in Monaco and Andorra, for they bring money to this tiny land.

Liechtenstein is probably the most well known of the storybook lands. It is located between Austria and Switzerland. The official language of Liechtenstein is German. About three hundred years ago the Liechtenstein family bought the land from a local count. That is how the country got its name. Liechtenstein is a constitutional monarchy, ruled by a prince of the Liechtenstein family.

Through the years, Liechtenstein has fallen into the hands of many different countries, but finally became allied with Switzerland. The same kind of money is used in both countries.

Liechtenstein is a prosperous country that makes money in a number of ways. Some of the people raise crops and animals for food; others are bankers who hold money for foreign investors. Liechtenstein also issues many kinds of stamps that are sought by collectors. This is another source of money for the country. There is some industry in Liechtenstein, and tourism is a big business. The country has many beautiful little hotels. Perhaps we should say that all the countries in Europe are storybook lands.

Wherever they live, the things people think and say and do are the things of which stories are made. Mountains, lowlands, plains, seas, and rivers are the settings for the action of the stories.

We call these settings geography. Knowing something about geography makes stories of the past and of the present much more interesting and meaningful than they otherwise would be. Sometimes geography itself gets into the action of a story. Stories would not be what they are without their settings.

INDEX: Young People's Story of Europe

Type   *Century Expanded*
Typesetter   *American Typesetting Corporation*
Printer   *The Regensteiner Corporation*